Prioritising Project Risks
A Short Guide to Useful Techniques

APM SIG GUIDES SERIES

Directing Change: A Guide to Governance of Project Management
ISBN: 978-1-903494-15-8

Co-Directing Change: A Guide to the Governance of Multi-Owned Projects
ISBN: 978-1-903494-94-3

Models to Improve the Management of Projects
ISBN: 978-1-903494-80-6

APM Introduction to Programme Management
ISBN: 978-1-903494-63-9

Interfacing Risk and Earned Value Management
ISBN: 978-1-903494-24-0

Introduction to Project Planning
ISBN: 978-1-903494-28-8

Earned Value Management
ISBN: 978-1-903494-26-4

Prioritising Project Risks
A Short Guide to Useful Techniques

edited by
Martin Hopkinson
Paul Close
David Hillson
Stephen Ward

on behalf of the
Risk Prioritisation Group

Association for Project Management

Association for Project Management
Ibis House, Regent Park
Summerleys Road, Princes Risborough
Buckinghamshire
HP27 9LE

British Library Cataloguing in Publication Data is available
ISBN 10: 1-903494-27-3
ISBN 13: 978-1-903494-27-1

Cover design by Mark Design
Typeset by RefineCatch Limited, Bungay, Suffolk
Printed by Ashford Colour Press Ltd., Gosport, Hants.
Copy editor: Merle Read
Publishing Manager: Ingmar Folkmans

Contents

Tables

Figures

Foreword

Everyone agrees that projects are risky, which is why risk management has become an integral part of the management of projects. However, projects are not equally risky, and not all risks deserve equal attention. Managers at all levels need to focus their efforts on managing the most important risks and the most risky projects.

An effective risk management process must include a sound approach to prioritisation of risks which recognises the challenges of dealing with the uncertainty associated with all risks. In many organisations, risk prioritisation is simplistic, using techniques which do not provide sufficient understanding of the risk exposure. Such techniques fail to support robust risk-based decision-making.

This guide addresses the shortfall in current practice by reviewing available techniques for prioritising project risks and making clear recommendations on when they should be used. A wide range of risk prioritisation methods are presented, and readers will find much here to help them make sense of the risk challenges they face. Prioritising project risks is not a simple matter, and there is no one-size-fits-all solution. However, careful and appropriate use of the techniques discussed in this guide will provide project managers and their stakeholders with a sound basis for prioritising and managing risks effectively.

Mike Nichols
Chair, Association for Project Management

Steve Fowler
CEO, Institute of Risk Management

Acknowledgements

This guide is the outcome of work undertaken by the Risk Prioritisation Group. The group was originally formed in response to earlier drafts of the paper by Chris Chapman (2006), 'Key Points of Contention in Framing Assumptions for Risk and Uncertainty Management', published in the *International Journal of Project Management* (Volume 24, Issue 4). It comprises project risk management professionals from a variety of backgrounds. Its membership, listed below, includes people with experience gained within companies, the public sector, academia and consultancy and risk tools developers.

Editing committee

Martin Hopkinson (Chair)	HVR Consulting Services Ltd
Paul Close	Fujitsu Services
David Hillson	Risk Doctor & Partners
Stephen Ward	University of Southampton

Other group members

Gordon Barr	HVR Consulting Services Ltd
Meredith Boden	Transport for London
Peter Campbell	HVR Consulting Services Ltd
Chris Chapman	University of Southampton
Karl Davey	Strategic Thought Group
Heather Groom	BEAR Analysts
Elaine Harris	De Montfort University
Guy Hindley	BAE Systems
David Hulett	Hulett & Associates
Matthew Leitch	Internal Controls Design
Ken Newland	Quintec Associates Ltd
Stephen Simister	Oxford Management & Research Ltd
Terry Williams	University of Southampton

The following techniques are original contributions not previously published:

- sliding windows extension to the probability–impact matrix, Section 4.1.3 (David Hillson);
- generalised multi-attribute approach to risk prioritisation, Section 4.2.1 (Paul Close);
- uncertainty–importance matrix, Section 4.2.4 (Martin Hopkinson);
- simple project risk re-estimating model, Section 4.3.7 (Chris Chapman).

1
Introduction

Project risk management addresses the implications of uncertainty for the project team, the sponsoring organisation, the users of the project's deliverables and other project stakeholders. The aim of this guide is to improve risk prioritisation by offering a choice of techniques ranging from simple to complex. Efficient prioritisation selects the simplest technique that will be suitable in the circumstances, but making the choice requires a clear understanding of why risks are being prioritised and what we mean by a risk.

Prioritisation is an important part of any risk process because it focuses attention on what matters most. However, 'what matters most' is variable in the sense that it depends on context. It varies from one stakeholder to another, and it changes during the course of the project, from one stage to another. For example, the most important impacts on the project sponsor at feasibility stage, before the project has been sanctioned, are not necessarily those that the project manager will regard as most important during project start-up. Additionally, the range of responses available to the project sponsor at feasibility stage will be typically much wider than those available to the project manager once the project has begun.

This variability of 'what matters most' raises questions in prioritisation, such as:

1. Where does the project team need to pay most attention to understanding risks in more detail?
2. What are the most important risks from the project sponsor's perspective?
3. How can the team identify those risks that should be prioritised for the implementation of risk responses?
4. How can quantitative risk models be used to identify key risks?
5. How can risks be prioritised if probability and impact cannot be reliably estimated?
6. Which risks threaten the feasibility of the project?

The third question above identifies an important distinction between prioritising risks and prioritising responses. This distinction is explored further in Section 3.

Prioritisation of risks is commonly associated with the assessment of probability and impact and the ranking of risks within a probability–impact matrix (PIM), so that risks with high impact and high probability assume the greatest importance. The familiarity of this technique leads us to assume that it is simple and effective, but probability and impact are not always easy to define or estimate. Nor are they always the most important attributes to consider.

Attempts to prioritise risks often raise another important question: what do we mean by risk? We know that uncertainty lies at the heart of risk. We also know that project risk can be complex, with many risk events and other sources of uncertainty contributing to the overall project risk. In this guide we have started from the concept of overall project risk. The APM *Project Risk Analysis and Management [PRAM] Guide* (2nd edition, 2004) describes project risk as resulting from 'an accumulation of a number of individual risk events, together with other sources of uncertainty to the project as a whole, such as variability and ambiguity'.

Types of risk that contribute towards overall project risk include:

- uncertainty concerning an event which, should it occur, would have an effect on the project objectives (event risks);
- uncertainty concerning the eventual value of an important project variable, including those that affect duration, cost and resource requirements (variability risks);
- uncertainty concerning the combined effect of multiple interdependent factors (systemic risks);
- uncertainty concerning the underlying understanding of the project (ambiguity risks).

Any of these types of risk can have a positive or negative impact on the project outcome. The project team may need to use the project risk management process to address either some or all of these types of uncertainty.

This guide also includes the concept of composite risks. These may comprise combinations of any or all of the risk types listed above. When using a multi-pass top-down approach to risk management, such as that recommended by the *PRAM Guide*, dealing with composite risks is an important part of the process, particularly during earlier passes. Composite risks might also be produced as a synthesis of contributory risks where it makes sense to do so, e.g. where an overarching response may be effective. The levels to which risk has been decomposed will, of course, affect prioritisation results. In addition, some techniques (including all of those related to quantitative modelling) cannot be expected to produce reliable prioritisation of risks unless risks have been understood within a coherent structure developed from a top-down perspective.

Finally, the scope of this guide also includes project strategy risks. Typically, these involve uncertainty about the fundamental role of the parties involved, the project objectives or factors that are critical to project success. Project strategy risks have the potential to change the purpose of a project or to fundamentally affect the way in which it is delivered.

Whatever scope is selected, the following are important aspects of risk prioritisation, often missing in common practice:

- risks should be understood before prioritising can begin;
- interrelationships between risks should be recognised, particularly in complex projects;
- risk management should begin in the earliest stages of a project;
- prioritisation, and the tools chosen to prioritise, should be part of a coherent process framework to analyse and manage risk in the project.

Section 2 addresses how we understand and describe risk. The purposes of risk prioritisation are explored in more detail in Section 3, and a selection of techniques to assist in prioritisation is presented in Section 4. The techniques selected in this guide are not intended to be exhaustive, and there may be other equally valid techniques available to projects. The techniques presented here have been chosen because they fulfil one or more of the following criteria:

- they are in common use;
- they are generally applicable;
- they give robust and reliable results;
- they are independent of proprietary tools.

Each of the techniques will be appropriate in some circumstances and not in others. The aim should be to select the simplest approach that will be suitable for the purpose of effective risk management. It is important to recognise in early passes of the prioritisation phase of the risk management process that there are sources of uncertainty that may require further analysis using more time-consuming and complex techniques. It is equally important to recognise where this is not necessary and avoid wasting time and resources on analysis of uncertainties that are of relatively low importance in terms of their effect on project objectives. These choices will almost certainly be more appropriate and effective if they are part of a coherent process framework.

It is important to recognise that there are significant differences of opinion about these choices, arising from different framing assumptions about the nature and scope of risk management. This guide attempts to clarify these differences and their effect on the choice of prioritisation technique.

2
Understanding and describing risks

Clear understanding of risks is an essential prerequisite for prioritising them; one cannot justify prioritising risks that have not been adequately understood. Risk descriptions are a vital tool for generating such understanding. A feature of good risk descriptions is that they include the information required both to make realistic estimates and to evaluate the relative importance of risks. Table 2.1 describes a number of risk attributes that might be taken into account when prioritising risks.

Of course not all the attributes shown in Table 2.1 will necessarily be relevant to risk prioritisation in any particular project or in any situation. But where these attributes are relevant they should be included in risk descriptions or related information such as descriptions of risk responses.

Table 2.1 Attributes that may be relevant to risk prioritisation

Risk attribute	Description
Probability	The probability that a risk will occur (note that risks that are not event risks may have a probability of 100%)
Impact	The consequence(s) or potential range of consequences of a risk should it occur
Impact – single dimension	Impact estimated in the dimension relevant to the context in which risk is being assessed (e.g. time or cost)
Variability	Uncertainty of outcome (typically evaluated as range or standard deviation)
Urgency	The nearness in time by which responses to a risk must be implemented in order for them to be effective
Proximity	The nearness in time at which a risk is expected or predicted to occur
Propinquity	The acuteness of a risk as perceived by either an individual or group
Controllability	The degree to which the risk's owner (or owning organisation) is able to control the risk's outcome

4

Risk attribute	Description
Response effectiveness	The degree to which current risk responses can be expected to influence a risk's outcome
Manageability	A function of controllability and response effectiveness
Relatedness	The degree to which causal relationships may correlate a risk's outcome with the outcome of other risks
Ownership ambiguity	The degree to which responsibility (either individual and/or organisational) for a risk's ownership lacks clarity

Given the importance of risk descriptions and the direct link to prioritisation, this guide describes a number of structured approaches that can be used to describe risks. Each of these structures differentiates between causal relationships that can be described in terms of facts and causal relationships characterised by uncertainty.

A commonly used simple structured risk description has three essential components: cause, risk and effect (see Figure 2.1). A *cause* is a certain event or set of circumstances that exists in the present, and that gives rise to one or more risks. A *risk* is an uncertain event or set of circumstances that might occur

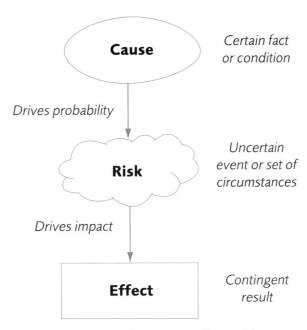

Figure 2.1 Simple cause–risk–effect model

in the future, and if it does occur it will affect achievement of one or more of the project's objectives. An *effect* is what would happen to achievement of the objectives when a risk occurs, and is also a future event, contingent on occurrence of the risk.

Use of a simple cause–risk–effect structure can be reflected in a three-part risk description (also known as 'risk metalanguage'), e.g. 'Because of <cause>, <risk> may occur, which would lead to <effect>.' The following example illustrates this format.

Example 1. Preferred electrical installation contractor unavailable. *Because the project's preferred supplier for electrical installation has a full order book, an alternative supplier may be required. This would lead to increased costs of 10% for the work involved.*

Two key parameters of risks are often used in prioritisation, namely *probability* and *impact*. Probability is a function of the cause–risk relationship, and the risk–effect relationship results in impact on objectives. The simple description of a risk using the cause–risk–effect framework therefore leads naturally to a prioritisation method based on probability and impact, and the standard probability–impact matrix (PIM) is an expression of that approach.

However, the cause–risk–effect model is a simplification that can be improved upon by expansion. Most projects have risks that are more complex than this, so it is a simplification that may not support effective risk prioritisation. There are several ways in which this model might be refined.

Firstly, the simple cause–risk–effect structure can be adapted, as in Figure 2.2. This recognises that some risks concern variability of effect rather than whether or not an effect will occur. All variability risks are of this nature, as are many ambiguity risks. In some cases, the risk impact could be either positive or negative relative to value assumed for a baseline. As with most risks, good descriptions of these risks require a sound understanding of relevant facts.

Examples 2 and 3 are risk descriptions based on the structure illustrated in Figure 2.2.

Example 2 (variability risk). Effect of exchange rates on costs of a foreign contract. *The supplier has provided a fixed price in foreign currency for the delivery of gas turbines. For planning purposes, the project budget has been set at the current exchange rate. However, uncertainty in future exchange rates will drive actual costs that may be either higher or lower than this baseline.*

Example 3 (ambiguity risk). Immature software specification. *The signal processing software specification is immature. It is uncertain how well aligned it is to the overall system specification. A detailed review can be expected to produce changes. An increase in software resource requirements can be expected, although these could range from three person-months to five person-years.*

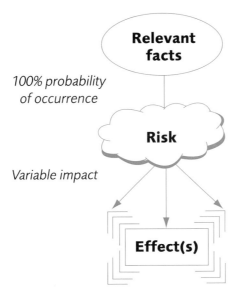

Figure 2.2 Model for risks concerned
only with variability of effect

It should be noted that a PIM is usually not a suitable tool for prioritising risks of this nature. Some organisations react to this problem by excluding the associated sources of uncertainty from their risk management process. This guide recommends that all significant sources of uncertainty should fall within the remit of the risk management process.

A more general model for risk descriptions can be developed by combining Figures 2.1 and 2.2. The model further broadens the idea of cause or relevant facts. For example, relevant facts could include assumptions or constraints, known vulnerabilities or decisions which will be required but have yet to be made. The probability of occurrence is influenced by one or more *risks*, i.e. sources of uncertainty. These sources of uncertainty may also drive the severity of the effect; where probability is 100%, understanding how the risks influence variation of effect is key to the overall risk description. This model more accurately reflects the relationships between the certain, uncertain and contingent elements. However, it is less easily reflected in the standard PIM, which cannot represent the full range of information.

Example 4 is a risk description based on the structure illustrated in Figure 2.3.

Example 4. Failure to co-locate software team. *It is planned that the software design team of 40 will be co-located in Reading within two months of contract*

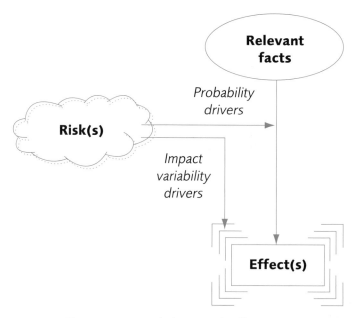

Figure 2.3 Expanded cause–risk–effect model

award. This may not be achieved, either because suitable facilities for the team cannot be established in time or because key members of the proposed software team refuse to relocate from their current base in Edinburgh. This would necessitate running the software team with its current geographic split, leading to requirements for additional effort and expenses to support communication, a parallel test environment to be set up and an estimated increase of between one and three months in the development phase due to inefficient working practices.

Example 4 illustrates how this risk description structure also provides a simple approach to describing composite risks. In this case two sources of uncertainty (time to establish facilities and the willingness of key people to move) influence a common effect. Both sources of uncertainty would have to be managed to mitigate the risk. From a risk prioritisation perspective it would therefore not make sense to decompose further by identifying the two sources of uncertainty as separate risks.

A further modification of the simple cause–risk–effect structure is a more complex but more flexible approach to describing composite risks. It expands each element into a network of links, recognising that in reality cause–risk–effect relationships are usually not singular (1:1:1) but multiple (many : many : many), as illustrated in Figure 2.4. This causal map can be useful in generating improved understanding of project risks. However, it is usually difficult to translate such insights into a simple two-dimensional PIM.

A key feature of the approach illustrated in Figure 2.4 is that it includes information about the relatedness of risks and the causes of this. It also shows how risk impacts can be described together as an aid to identify common effects. Insights into these features of risks are often important to quantitative modelling of overall project risk, and hence also to the use of quantitative modelling techniques for risk prioritisation purposes.

Causal mapping is also often useful when understanding project strategy risks. Example 5 is a project strategy risk since it concerns decisions about the project objectives. The example given is a summary of a more detailed description.

Example 5. Time and cost to build a new assembly facility. *The change to production capability to be delivered by the project will require a new assembly facility to be built. Key risks to the time and cost for the new facility include planning permission, purchase of new land (if required), procurement of production machinery and management decisions, yet to be made, in respect of the facility's capacity. Planning permission is likely to be achieved more easily if the new facility is accommodated within the current premises, but this would constrain its capacity below the limits initially indicated as ideal by the project sponsor.*

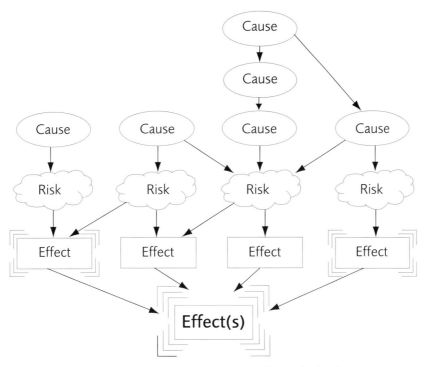

Figure 2.4 Causal map showing cause–risk–effect multiple relationships

Another view of the cause–risk–effect situation is reflected in the influence diagram of Figure 2.5, which includes the effect of risk responses. A key benefit of understanding risk is that it enables the identification of effective responses. It should also be noted that three of the risk attributes that affect prioritisation decisions shown in Table 2.1 (controllability, response effectiveness and manageability) can only be understood when there is good understanding of the availability, nature and status of risk responses.

While this technique may offer a rich description of risk prioritisation drivers, the process of risk prioritisation becomes more complicated, and a standard PIM cannot be used.

In conclusion, prioritisation of project risks based on cause–risk–effect alone is not as simple as is commonly thought. When the basic structure illustrated in Figure 2.1 is expanded in various ways to be more realistic, the risk prioritisation process starts to raise more complex problems.

As a result there is a need for other prioritisation techniques which reflect reality at an appropriate level (i.e. which are neither too simplistic nor overly complex), which take proper account of risk attributes other than just probability and impact, and which provide a clear focus on the most risky areas of the project.

It is important for any reliable prioritisation technique to cope with all types of risk encountered on projects, including those outlined in Section 1, namely: event risks, variability risks, systemic risks, ambiguity risks, composite risks and project strategy risks. The standard PIM approach may be suitable in some circumstances for some of these risk types, and it may be possible to modify

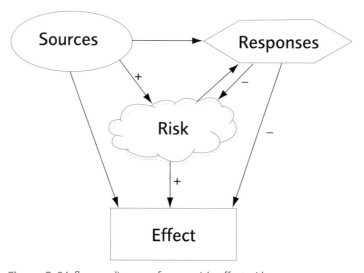

Figure 2.5 Influence diagram of cause–risk–effect with responses

the PIM technique to cope with other risk types. However, there are some types of risk for which the PIM is inherently unsuitable, and for which other prioritisation techniques are required.

This section has illustrated how risk attributes relevant to prioritisation can be included in risk descriptions. Section 3 continues by showing that the prioritisation process may itself have different purposes. The use of risk attributes for prioritisation purposes therefore depends upon the context in which prioritisation is conducted.

3

Purposes of
risk prioritisation

There are essentially two reasons to prioritise project risks: (1) to inform stake-holders of the range of outcomes arising from uncertainty, and (2) to prioritise risk responses for the effective management of risk.

3.1 PRIORITISATION OF RISKS

Prioritising helps to identify risk that matters (i.e. the range of outcomes of a particular risk or the project in its entirety) to major stakeholders, and to support decision-making and escalation and consideration of possible responses to individual risks or particular outcomes.

For example, broad variability of project completion date may be acceptable but a high budget overrun may not be so: therefore the major perceived causes of budget overrun must be identified so that they can be addressed or investigated further. The causes of timescale variability may not warrant further investigation if the range of expected outcomes is acceptable. Detailed modelling of project task durations would be inappropriate in this case, but detailed modelling of some areas of budget and contingency may be required.

Prioritisation of risks requires an understanding of risk attributes (see Table 2.1), such as probability, variability, impact, relatedness, propinquity, ownership ambiguity, and manageability, to assess the main risk events or outcomes that must be addressed for the project to be regarded as successful against its objectives and constraints. Prioritisation of risks also identifies uncertainties where further investigation would be relevant to understand the extent of the uncertainty.

3.2 PRIORITISATION OF RESPONSES

Prioritisation of responses informs decisions about what is to be done, when and by whom, for the project manager and the project sponsor. Prioritisation of responses requires understanding of attributes such as urgency, proximity, controllability and response effectiveness in order to execute the actions effectively and in a timely manner for the best return on available resources.

3.3 APPLYING RISK PRIORITISATION IN PROJECT MANAGEMENT

Throughout the project life-cycle, from feasibility to closure, the project sponsor and project manager will be asking questions such as:

1. What is the current situation?
2. What needs to be done and why?
3. Do we want to do it?
4. What would we do and how (high level)?
5. What will we do and how (detail)?
6. Are we doing it right?
7. How well did we do?

Prioritisation of risk relates to these questions as shown in Table 3.1.

Throughout the project there is a close relationship between the project's estimation processes and risk prioritisation. Risk prioritisation may be part of

Table 3.1 Risk prioritisation questions

Question	Purpose of risk prioritisation
1. What is the current situation?	Clarifying and sizing uncertainty and the effects of risks
2. What needs to be done and why?	Clarifying uncertainty about ambiguity and project strategy risks
3. Do we want to do it?	Clarifying expectations and variability in respect of overall project risk
4. What would we do and how (high level)?	Capturing and evaluating uncertainty to support exploring and choosing strategic options
5. What will we do and how (detail)?	Capturing and evaluating uncertainty to support exploring and choosing tactical options and implementation detail
6. Are we doing it right?	Managing risk to which the project is still exposed
7. How well did we do?	Identifying useful lessons learned

the estimation process, and unbiased estimation may be an essential part of risk prioritisation.

The most appropriate technique for prioritisation at a particular stage of the process depends on the nature and degree of detail of information that is available at that stage and the level of estimating confidence.

The applicability of each of the techniques described in Section 4 to each of the questions above is shown in Table 5.1 in Section 5.

4
Prioritisation techniques

This section describes a variety of risk management techniques. Some are high-level techniques designed to deal with risks identified primarily from a top-down perspective. These are often of greatest value in the earliest phases of a project. Others become more applicable as project information becomes increasingly detailed. Anyone wishing to prioritise risks should aim to choose the simplest techniques that are appropriate given the data available, while avoiding the trap of choosing techniques that are simplistic.

The techniques have been divided into three groups. Section 4.1 includes techniques that focus exclusively on the risk attributes of probability and impact. By comparing the combination of these attributes on a risk-by-risk basis, these techniques are designed to prioritise risks within the context of a list of risks or a risk register. Section 4.2 includes techniques that also adopt a risk-by-risk prioritisation approach. However, they use a variety of methods to broaden the perspective of risk prioritisation with a fuller range of risk attributes from among those listed in Table 2.1. Section 4.3 includes techniques that can be used to prioritise risks quantitatively within a model that represents the combined effects of risks to levels up to and including the analysis of overall project risk. This section also illustrates how risk prioritisation can be used to choose how and where to focus attention during successive iterations of a best-practice risk management process.

Each risk prioritisation technique is described under the following headings:

- purpose and applicability;
- description;
- examples;
- references (where appropriate).

4.1 PRIORITISING RISKS USING PROBABILITY AND IMPACT

4.1.1 Probability–impact picture

Purpose and applicability

The probability–impact picture (PIP) offers a flexible format for depicting independent event risks, variability risks and ambiguity risks. When event risks are involved, it allows specification of a range for the probability of occurrence, and a range for the impact should the risk event occur. The former recognises the often highly subjective nature of probability estimates. The latter recognises that the size of impact, should an event occur, is usually uncertain. The PIP allows the relative sizing of event risks in a more transparent manner than the probability–impact matrix (see Section 4.1.2), by showing the uncertainty about probability and impact estimates for each risk. But most important, it facilitates comparison of variability and ambiguity risks as well as event risks.

Description

1. Select an impact dimension and units in which the impact is to be specified.
2. For each risk, estimate the range for the probability of some level of impact occurring by specifying a pessimistic and optimistic probability of occurrence. Call these P_p and P_o. For variability or ambiguity (ever-present) risks, such as weather or market conditions or no design as yet, or no contract as yet, or no agreed specification as yet, set $P_p = P_o = 1$.
3. For each risk, estimate the range of possible impacts assuming the risk occurs by specifying a pessimistic and optimistic size of impact. Call these I_p and I_o.
4. For each risk, plot on a probability–impact graph the rectangle $(I_oP_o, I_oP_p, I_pP_o, I_pP_p)$. This denotes the range of possible combinations of probability of occurrence and impact.
5. Various simple prioritising rules might be applied to the PIP. For example, attend first to risks with: the highest absolute value of I_p, then P_p values for risks with similar values of I_p; the highest absolute I_pP_p values; or the risks with the largest rectangles $(I_oP_o, I_oP_p, I_pP_o, I_pP_p)$.

Example 1

There are three possible sources of delay to a project: (a) weather, (b) suppliers and (c) equipment. Associated risks and estimates of probability and impact are shown in Table 4.1, and plotted in Figure 4.1.

A simplification would be to plot the centre points of rectangles for risks (a), (b) and (c) in Figure 4.1 onto a PIM. However, this clearly ignores important information about the uncertainty present. In Figure 4.1, the relative importance of each risk is more equivocal, and risks with a probability of 1 have a role to play. This highlights the different nature of each, and the desirability of influencing each in different ways for different reasons.

Table 4.1 Probability and impact ranges for the estimates made for three risks

Risk	Event probability		Impact (days lost)	
	Pessimistic P_p	Optimistic P_o	Pessimistic I_p	Optimistic I_o
(a) Weather	1	1	12	2
(b) Late arrival of supplies	0.2	0.0	8	0
(c) Equipment failure	0.7	0.5	8	6

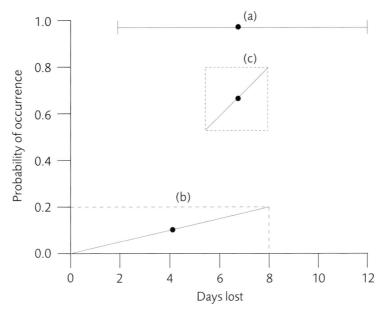

Figure 4.1 Mapping of three risks onto a probability–impact picture (PIP)

Example 2

This example illustrates the following four ways in which the core PIP technique shown in Example 1 can be extended if appropriate:

- the introduction of an explicit opportunity side to the impact dimension, beyond the good weather aspects of the weather risk in Example 1 – this allows variability, ambiguity and composite risks to be depicted that straddle the threat/opportunity divide;

- explicit consideration of composite risks;
- the addition of guidelines showing boundaries of equivalent expected value (calculated as probability × impact);
- reduction of the rectangles to lines between the points (I_oP_p, I_pP_o) or (I_oP_o, I_pP_p). Depicting an event risk by the line (I_oP_o, I_pP_p) would be appropriate if it were felt that the more likely an event to occur, the worse its impact would be. Depicting an event risk by the line (I_oP_p, I_pP_o) would be appropriate if it were felt that the more likely an event to occur, the less its impact would be. This latter view would apply where an estimator considers certain risks to have a high probability of a low impact, but lower probability of a high impact.

As part of a major infrastructure maintenance project, a railway company is investing in the procurement of a new wagon type. Following a competitive tendering process for the design and manufacture of the new wagons, an overseas supplier has been selected. This has secured a fixed price for the delivery of wagons to the railway company's specification, providing that the order is placed prior to a specified validity date. The client's risks retained by the railway company are shown in Table 4.2. The risks detailed in Table 4.2 are illustrated in the PIP shown in Figure 4.2. Note that where there is more than

Table 4.2 Railway wagon procurement risks

Risk	Probability (%)		Cost impact (£K)	
	P_o	P_p	I_o	I_p
A Price change should validity expire	10	50	500	1500
B Change to axle weight specification	50	80	1000	3000
C Change in safety regulations	30	30	1500	3000
D Project management costs	100	100	−500	−1000
E Exchange rate variation	100	100	−3000	3000
F Reduced number of wagons	50	10	−3000	−1000

NB: No commas in nos here but are in later tables

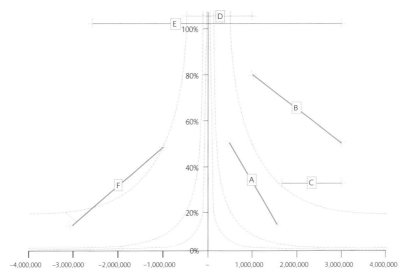

Figure 4.2 PIP showing railway wagon procurement risks

one risk with a probability of 100% (i.e. a composite risk or a variability risk or an ambiguity risk), these risks can be depicted by stacking them above the 100% probability level. A prioritisation order for the risks could be judged to be E, B, C, F, D, A.

Reference

Chapman, C.B. and Ward, S.C. (2003) *Project Risk Management: Processes, Techniques and Insights*, 2nd edition, John Wiley, Chichester, ch. 15.

4.1.2 Probability–Impact Matrix

Purpose and applicability

A probability–impact matrix is used to produce a relative ranking of risk events, by combining measures of probability (expressed as the percentage likelihood of occurrence or frequency) and impact (in one or more dimensions, e.g. cost, timescale, reputation). The PIM can be used for threats and opportunities.

The matrix can be used to determine a P–I score for each risk event, enabling the events to be prioritised, and to plot the risk events to provide a graphical representation (often known as a risk map or risk profile).

The PIM approach assumes that the project is dealing with independent risk events whose probability and impact can be assessed to within the limits of a band on the scale. This approach is not suitable for prioritising all sources of uncertainty, such as variability of outcome, and does not take account of inter-dependence between risks, where a common cause or a domino effect would lead to different priorities where these factors are apparent. For example, a relatively small time impact in a task on the critical path of a project may have a direct impact on the project end date and be worthy of greater priority than a longer time impact on a non-critical task.

The PIM does not take into account any of the other prioritisation factors listed in Section 2, such as the urgency or proximity of the risk, so is unsuitable (on its own) for prioritising actions.

The PIM can lead to prioritisation outcomes that are not appropriate. For example, very low probability but very high impact threats may be given lower prioritisation than would be preferred.

It is important that these other uncertainties and risk factors are not ignored or forgotten.

Description

The PIM is one of the most common and familiar prioritisation techniques. Some thought should be given to setting up the PIM before it is used and ensuring that the matrix is used as intended.

Setting up the matrix

Each of the two axes is split into a number of bands, each representing a scale of values. For example, probability and impact could each be split into five bands as shown in Figure 4.3. Each division is allocated an 'Index'. For a given

Probability	0.9	VHI	0.045	0.09	0.18	0.36	0.72
	0.7	HI	0.035	0.07	0.14	0.28	0.56
	0.5	MED	0.025	0.05	0.10	0.20	0.40
	0.3	LO	0.015	0.03	0.06	0.12	0.24
	0.1	VLO	0.005	0.01	0.02	0.04	0.08
			VLO	LO	MED	HI	VHI
			0.05	0.1	0.2	0.4	0.8
			Impact				

Figure 4.3 Example of PIM indices

20

risk, the P–I score can be determined from the intersection of the row and column relating to the probability and impact bands.

An important adjunct to the PIM is a clear definition of the meaning of the bands on each scale, and it may be convenient to include an impact definitions table (as in Figure 4.4), along with any rules for combining impacts (for example, if the schedule impact, project cost and product performance impacts are judged to be different, then take the worst case), alongside the PIM.

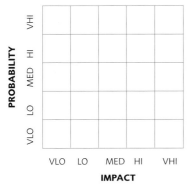

SCALE	PROBABILITY	+/– IMPACT ON PROJECT OBJECTIVES		
		TIME	COST	QUALITY
VHI	>70%	>4 months	>£250K	Very significant impact on overall functionality
HI	51–70%	2–4 months	£101K– £250K	Significant impact on overall functionality
MED	21–50%	1–2 months	£51K– £100K	Some impact in key functional areas
LO	5–20%	1–4 weeks	£10K– £50K	Minor impact on overall functionality
VLO	<5%	<1 week	<£10K	Minor impact on secondary functions

Figure 4.4 Example of a traditional 5×5 PIM

It is important that the relative priorities of the objectives are reflected in the impact definitions. For example, for a time-constrained project with a fixed end date, an impact of a few days' slippage may be regarded as HI or VHI.

A notional line may be drawn on the matrix to indicate the area where risks must be proactively managed.

When a PIM has been created it tends to be reused without question, but the size of the matrix and the values can be adjusted. A 3×3 matrix is often regarded as too coarse for a mature project, but can be appropriate during the early stages of the project or feasibility stage when a crude risk 'triage' is required. Later in the project, as estimates of impact and probabilities become more clearly defined and reliable, a 4×4 or 5×5 matrix may be more appropriate to prevent clustering of many of the risks in one cell of the matrix.

The values on the PIM can be manipulated, using a non-linear scale, to produce a 'skew' towards impact or probability. When using the PIM for both threats and opportunities, an exact mirror-image may not be appropriate for the prioritisation of opportunities, so an asymmetric matrix may be required.

Using the PIM

The P–I index for a risk is determined by assessing the appropriate impact and probability band for the risk and taking the number that is shown at the

Probability						
0.9	VHI	0.045	0.09	0.18	0.36	0.72
0.7	HI	0.035	0.07	0.14	0.28	0.56
0.5	MED	0.025	0.05	0.10	0.20	0.40
0.3	LO	0.015	0.03	0.06	0.12	0.24
0.1	VLO	0.005	0.01	0.02	0.04	0.08
		VLO	LO	MED	HI	VHI
		0.05	0.1	0.2	0.4	0.8
				Impact		

Figure 4.5 Identification of the P–I index for a medium-probability/low-impact risk

intersection of the two bands. In Figure 4.5 a risk with medium probability and low impact has a P–I index of 0.05 (the product of the 0.5 value for MED on the probability scale and the 0.1 value for LO on the impact scale).

The index can be used to put the risks into priority order and/or plot the risks on a grid similar to that shown in Figure 4.6 to provide a visual risk map for the project. The matrix can also be used to define the area of attention for threats

				Arrow of Attention						

		Threats						**Opportunities**					
0.9	VHI	0.045	0.09	0.18	0.36	0.72	0.72	0.36	0.18	0.09	0.045	0.9	VHI
0.7	HI	0.035	0.07	0.14	0.28	0.56	0.56	0.28	0.14	0.07	0.035	0.7	HI
0.5	MED	0.025	0.05	0.10	0.20	0.40	0.40	0.20	0.10	0.05	0.025	0.5	MED
0.3	LO	0.015	0.03	0.06	0.12	0.24	0.24	0.12	0.06	0.03	0.015	0.3	LO
0.1	VLO	0.005	0.01	0.02	0.04	0.08	0.08	0.04	0.02	0.01	0.005	0.1	VLO
		VLO	LO	MED	HI	VHI	VHI	HI	MED	LO	VLO		
		0.05	0.1	0.2	0.4	0.8	0.8	0.4	0.2	0.1	0.05		
				Impact					Benefit				

Probability (left axis) — Probability (right axis)

Figure 4.6 Example of a risk-prioritisation scheme combining threats and opportunities

that may exceed the project tolerance and opportunities that should be actively managed.

The P–I value is a relative index and should only be used with care for any other computation.

It is essential that users of the PIM are aware of the threshold values for the bands and allocate the risks accordingly. However, in the early stages of a project it may be difficult to assess both impact and probability. Reassessment of the risks and their P–I values should be carried out regularly.

Planned responses to risks will lead to an expected change in probability, impact or both. A consistent approach must be taken as to which of the values (before or after the introduction of responses) is used when determining the P–I score.

References

APM (2004) *Project Risk Analysis and Management Guide*, 2nd edition, APM Publishing, High Wycombe, ISBN 1-903494-12-5.
PMI (2004) *A Guide to the Project Management Body of Knowledge (PMBOK)*, 3rd edition, Project Management Institute, Pennsylvania.

4.1.3 PIM extension using sliding windows

Purpose and applicability

The PIM extension using sliding windows addresses one of the perceived shortfalls of the traditional probability–impact matrix, namely insufficient granularity in the outermost scale points. It can be used wherever a traditional PIM is considered appropriate. The technique is particularly useful at programme or portfolio levels, when an organisation wishes to show risks of various types in a single visual format. This presentation also defines overlaps between areas of interest at different levels in an organisation, recognising for example that a 'high' impact at project level might only be deemed 'low' at programme level. Its particular strength is the ability to show very wide ranges of probability and impacts on a single diagram.

Description

The traditional PIM is usually symmetrical: for example, 3×3 or 5×5. It also often uses 'less than' and 'greater than' at its extremes, as shown in Figure 4.4, which presents a 5×5 PIM with associated definitions for 'VLO/LO/ MED/HI/ VHI' for both probability and impacts.

This introduces a limitation to the traditional PIM, since, for example, impacts of £251,000 and £1M both fall in the >£250K position. Some organisations may wish to show finer differentiation than is allowed by the traditional PIM. This can be achieved by extending the impact dimension to left and right to give additional definition at the ends of the scale, as shown in Figure 4.7.

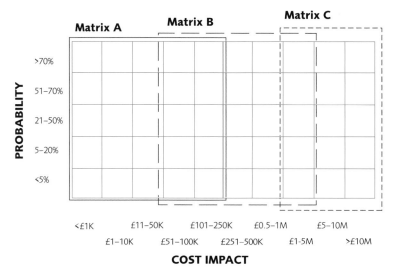

Figure 4.7 Use of the 'sliding window' to increase granularity of impact classification

This technique is known as the sliding window since it is possible to generate a number of smaller PIMs from the wider matrix, simply by selecting a view that is appropriate to the level under consideration. So in the example shown in Figure 4.7, a project perspective may be interested in impacts ranging from £1,000 to £250,000, so the PIM for project risk management can be defined as Matrix A in the figure. Programme-level impacts may lie in the range ≠0.5–5M, so Matrix B might form the programme risk management PIM. A strategic risk assessment might use Matrix C. The overlap between these matrices also defines where risks should be escalated/delegated from one level to the next.

The basic sliding window PIM is produced simply by extending the impact range to left and right. It is also possible to extend the probability range similarly, to allow different types of risk to be represented. For example, in project risk management, a 'low probability' risk may be defined as having probability less than 1%. For risks with safety impact, 1% probability of occurrence might be deemed 'high'. Extending both probability and impact ranges to produce a generic PIM allows the organisation to define a range of 'views of interest' within the grid, as shown in Figure 4.8.

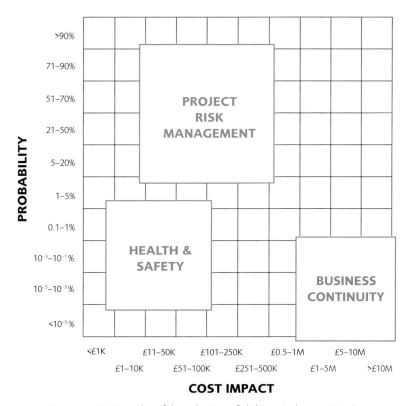

Figure 4.8 Examples of the selection of sliding window positioning

4.1.4 Summary statistics of probability distributions: expected value

Purpose and applicability

One way of sizing individual sources of risk is to order them with respect to size of expected impact. In a given impact dimension, such as cost, expected impact is calculated by multiplying each possible impact by its associated probability of occurrence and summing. This gives a weighted average of the impact from a source of risk that takes into account all the possible estimated outcomes. For risks with possible impacts which are either only adverse (i.e. all threats) or only beneficial (all opportunities), expected impact might be regarded as a relatively simple method of comparing the size of different sources of risk.

25

Description

1. The impact dimension and units in which to calculate expected values and standard deviations should be selected, e.g. the cost impact dimension with units in £K.
2. The probability and impact estimates for each risk should be translated into a probability density function using the selected impact dimension and units.
3. Expected value is calculated. In cases of risk events where there is some probability of non-occurrence (and hence no impact), it can be more convenient to first estimate the probability density function of impact assuming some impact occurs, that is the *conditional* probability distribution, and then calculate the expected value of this distribution (that is the *conditional* expected value). The required *unconditional* expected value is then obtained by multiplying the conditional expected value by the probability of the event occurring.
4. Risks are then ranked in order of unconditional expected value on the chosen impact dimension.
5. This approach might be extended to sources of risk quantified in more than one dimension (for example cost and time) either by considering sets of expected values for each source, or by converting expected values onto a common value scale. In practice this may not be worthwhile, especially if the impact dimensions are highly interdependent.

Example

Sources of risk A, B, C are estimated to have the potential cost impacts on a project detailed in Table 4.3. For convenience assume that the conditional probability density functions of impacts for A, B, and C are all triangular and are defined by the three-point estimates in the table. Then the conditional expected value is given by (minimum + most likely + maximum)/3. Ranking according to expected value implies a prioritisation of C, A and then B.

Table 4.3 Expected value calculations made on the basis of estimates for three risks (I)

| Risk | Probability of event | Possible cost of impact | | | Conditional expected value | Unconditional expected value |
		Minimum	Most likely	Maximum		
A	1.0	10	20	30	20	20
B	0.4	10	20	30	20	8
C	0.8	20	40	90	50	40

4.1.5 Variance/standard deviation

Purpose and applicability

Comparing expected values of impact for individual sources of risk fails to adequately consider the variability of possible impacts. In contrast, a risk's variance can be a better measure of the degree to which there is uncertainty about its outcome. Using variance (σ^2) as a measure also allows all risks that can be mapped onto a probability–impact picture (PIP) to be compared, including those risks that straddle the opportunity/threat divide. However, standard deviation (σ) derived from variance also achieves this and is a more commonly understood, and thus preferred, measure. It also provides a more useful numerical point of comparison with expected value (E).

Description

1. The impact dimension and units in which to calculate expected values and standard deviations should be selected, e.g. the cost impact dimension with units in £K.
2. The probability and impact estimates for each risk should be translated into a probability density function using the selected impact dimension and units.
3. Calculate the variance or standard deviation for each risk. Note that these calculations should be based on the whole of each probability density function, including the element that describes the risk's probability of having zero impact.
4. Rank risks in descending order of variance or standard deviation.

Example

Sources of risk A, B, C, D and E are estimated to have the potential cost impacts on a project detailed in Table 4.4 (negative values are shown in brackets). Standard deviations have been calculated using an independent Monte Carlo simulation for each risk.

Risks A, B and C are the same risks as used for the previous expected value example (see Table 4.3). For convenience assume that the conditional probability density functions of impacts for the additional risks D and E are also triangular. All impact values of E are negative, showing that it is an opportunity. D is a variability risk that straddles the threat/opportunity divide.

On the basis of expected value, the risks are ranked C, A, B, E, D. However, when standard deviation is used, the significance of Risk D's variance becomes more apparent. In comparison, the significance of Risk A declines. This reflects

27

Table 4.4 Expected value calculations made on the basis
of estimates for three risks (II)

Risk	Probability of event	Possible cost of impact			Expected value	Standard Deviation
		Minimum	Most likely	Maximum		
A	1.0	10	20	30	20	4.1
B	0.4	10	20	30	8	10.2
C	0.8	20	40	90	40	23.9
D	1.0	(60)	(5)	50	(5)	22.5
E	0.2	(50)	(30)	(10)	(6)	12.6

the low degree of uncertainty associated with Risk A, whose high expected value is attributable to a 100% probability of having an impact greater than zero. On the basis of standard deviations, the risks are ranked C, D, E, B, A.

Combining expected value and standard deviation

Sources of risk could be sized and compared according to both expected value and standard deviation. Using two summary statistics to describe the underlying probability distribution of impacts for each source of risk makes use of two measures of a risk's 'size', either of which could be indicative of its significance.

If $E_A > E_B$ and $\sigma_A \geq \sigma_B$ then A is a higher priority risk than B (note that, if opportunities are included, modular values of E should be used, to remove negatives).

However, a difficulty of using this approach lies in resolving situations of ambiguity between the two measures. For example, if $E_A > E_B$ and $\sigma_A \leq \sigma_B$, then individual judgement must be used to decide which should be the higher priority risk, or that both should be of equal priority. If a pair of risks had similar values according to one measure, but significantly different values on the basis of another, then it would be reasonable to use the latter to resolve the prioritisation ambiguity.

4.2 PRIORITISING RISKS USING MULTI-ATTRIBUTE TECHNIQUES

4.2.1 Generalised multi-attribute risk prioritisation

Purpose and applicability

Twelve attributes of risk are described in Table 2.1. This approach enables several of them to be considered together for the purpose of prioritisation.

This approach can be used for qualitatively defined strategic risks or very detailed quantitative risks by appropriate selection of criteria and definition of assessment thresholds. Probability can be omitted or replaced by variability. The approach can be used for both threats and opportunities.

Description

The attributes of interest (e.g. as in Table 4.5) for a particular analysis are selected, on the basis of the purpose of the prioritisation, the interests of the stakeholder and the level of information available at this stage of the project. For each attribute, a criterion table must be defined as for a PIM. The tables may be a crude triage (e.g. high/medium/low) or a finer scale to suit the project stage and the type of attributes selected.

From this table, priorities can be decided by stakeholders according to their own rules. For example, a score of 5 against any criterion can mark the risk as a 'priority' risk, or an arithmetic formula can be used to calculate an overall

Table 4.5 Example of ratings for different prioritisation categories

Risks	Probability	Impact (time)	Impact (cost)	Proximity	Varia-bility	Rela-tedness	Manage-ability	Response effectiveness
Risk 1	2	4	0	1	0	0	2	4
Risk 2	3	3	0	2	0	0	1	3
Risk 3	1	2	0	3	0	0	2	2
Risk 4	4	1	0	4	0	0	1	1
Risk 5	5	2	0	5	0	0	1	1
Risk 6	2	3	0	2	0	0	1	4

priority index, applying weighting to the criteria if required. If arithmetic formulae are to be used, they should be treated with caution and tested thoroughly against a number of scenarios to ensure that the calculation works as expected.

There is clearly more effort and thought required to tailor an approach of this type than there is to use a standard PIM, but it does encourage some thought to be given to the reasons for prioritisation and selection of attributes: therefore a more suitable prioritised list is likely to result for the effort expended.

4.2.2 Bubble chart

Purpose and applicability

The bubble chart allows three characteristics of a risk to be shown in a single graphical format on an *x/y* plot with circles of differing size.

Description

Bubble charts are used in a range of applications outside risk management to show three dimensions on a single chart, with two being represented on the *x*- and *y*-axes respectively, and a third being indicated by the size of a circular 'bubble'. They were originally used for risk prioritisation as part of the assumption-based communication dynamics (ABCD) risk methodology, but they have been adopted and adapted more widely.

Various sets of three characteristics can be shown in a bubble chart, as shown in Table 4.6, for example: It is common for the axis scales to be oriented so that risks which are to be given higher priority 'bubble up' to the top of the chart. However, some versions have high-priority risks 'sinking' to be close to the origin.

Table 4.6 Examples of risk characteristics illustrated by bubble charts

X-axis	Y-axis	Bubble size
Probability	Impact	Manageability
P–I score	Action window	Manageability
Urgency	Manageability	Impact value

Examples

Two example bubble charts are shown in Figures 4.9 and 4.10. The first example has high-priority risks in the top-right-hand corner, with high urgency, low manageability and high impact value, while Figure 4.10 shows high-priority risks plotted near the origin, because they have high criticality, high urgency and low controllability.

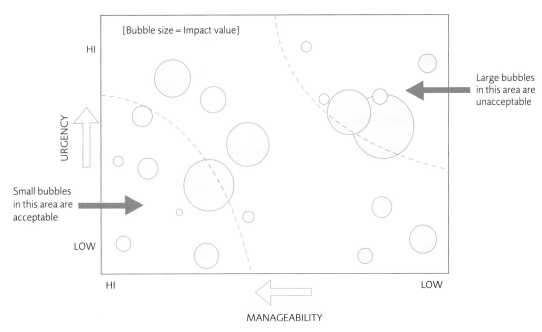

Figure 4.9 Example bubble chart (I), showing high-priority risks in upper right

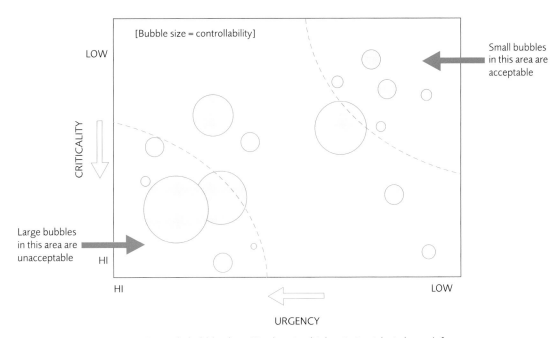

Figure 4.10 Example bubble chart (II), showing high-priority risks in lower left

4.2.3 Risk prioritisation chart

Purpose and applicability

A variety of characteristics can be used to prioritise risks. The risk prioritisation chart allows three different dimensions to be shown in a single graphical format. The first two of these are usually used to represent probability and impact, but the third dimension can show one of a range of factors. Examples of the third dimension for which this technique is particularly useful include urgency (risk response window), impact window, response cost, manageability and propinquity.

Description

The risk prioritisation chart typically has probability and impact in the vertical (y) axis, plotted above and below the horizontal (x) axis line respectively. The x-axis is used for the third dimension.

The risks having been plotted on the risk prioritisation chart, a sensitivity threshold can be added. Risks which cut the threshold in both vertical directions are prioritised for management attention. The threshold could be stepped to reflect specific values relevant to the project, or it might be linear.

Table 4.7 Data for example risk prioritisation chart in Figure 4.11

Risk	Probability	Impact	Urgency
R1	M	M	<1 week
R2	L	L	<1 week
R3	VL	M	<1 week
R4	M	H	<1 week
R5	L	VL	<1 week
R6	M	M	<1 week
R7	H	H	1–4 weeks
R8	VL	M	1–4 weeks
R9	L	H	1–4 weeks
R10	H	VL	1–4 weeks
R11	M	M	1–3 months
R12	VL	H	1–3 months

Example

The example of a risk prioritisation chart given here (Figure 4.11) shows probability and impact in the vertical dimension, with urgency in the third (horizontal) dimension, and plots the risks shown in Table 4.7. In this example, probability and impacts are rated as VL/L/M/H, though numerical values can be used (e.g. percentage for probability, and weeks or a currency for impact). Urgency is also given in ranges, though specific values can also be used. Plotting these risks in Figure 4.11 results in the prioritisation of risks R1, R4, R6 and R7.

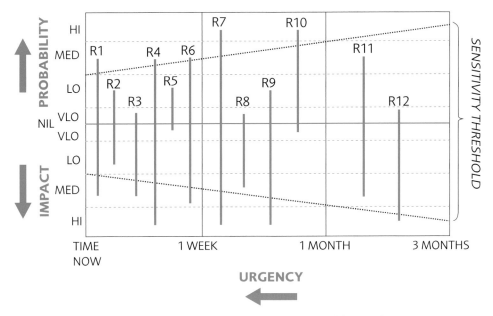

Figure 4.11 Example risk prioritisation chart (adapted from Barber, 2003)

Reference

Barber, R.B. (2003) 'A Systems Toolbox for Risk Management,' Proceedings of ANZSYS Conference, Monash, Australia, November 2003

4.2.4 Uncertainty–importance matrix

Purpose and applicability

The uncertainty–importance matrix (UIM) is consistent with the broad concept of a project risk as described in Section 1. It is based on the principle that all risks are characterised by uncertainty and that the highest priority risks are those for which the uncertainties involved are liable to be of greatest importance to the project. In this context uncertainty should be taken to mean 'lack of certainty'. The technique is at its most effective during the earliest phases of a project when there is insufficient definition of strategy and plans to make impact assessments on the basis of deviation from objectives. After this point, other techniques are likely to provide more objective grounds for prioritisation. However, a UIM may also be valuable later if the prevailing risk management process is considered to lack breadth.

Description

Attributes of risks that are relevant to prioritisation can be considered to contribute towards either uncertainty or its implications in terms of its importance to the project. Table 4.8 illustrates this using the risk attributes from Table 2.1.

The steps required to use an uncertainty–importance matrix are as follows.

1. Identify which risk attributes are relevant to the purposes of prioritisation.
2. Develop working definitions for levels of uncertainty and importance (i.e. the labels used to delineate the cells in the UIM).
3. Map each risk to the UIM using the highest combination of uncertainty and importance.
4. Where two indicators of uncertainty are assessed as having an equal level, map the overall level of uncertainty for the risk as being at the next level higher. This recommendation is made on the grounds that the uncertainties involved are likely to be complex.

Table 4.8 Risk attributes indicative of uncertainty and importance

Attributes indicative of uncertainty	Attributes indicative of whether or not the uncertainty is important to the project
• Uncertainty of occurrence • Variability • Ownership ambiguity	• Impact (in single or multiple dimensions) • Urgency • Proximity • Propinquity • Controllability • Response effectiveness • Manageability • Relatedness

Example

A hospital trust has authorised a concept phase study for a project that would amalgamate services currently delivered at three separate hospitals, potentially at a single site. The factors considered to be most relevant to prioritising risks include uncertainty concerning objectives and risk ownership, impact on outcomes, risk response urgency and manageability. These factors are used to construct a UIM, as shown in Figure 4.12. This figure also shows three risks that have been mapped:

- Risk A – the public response to the project;
- Risk B – the impact of the project on ambulance service logistics;
- Risk C – the contracting strategy for project delivery.

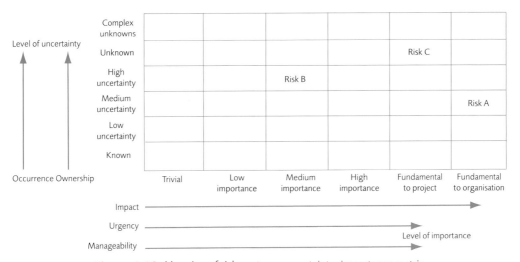

Figure 4.12 Mapping of risks onto an uncertainty–importance matrix

A UIM may help to classify risks and select them for escalation purposes. Figure 4.13 illustrates the ways in which different types of risk are likely to be mapped. This figure also shows that the UIM differentiates between risks and planning issues. Projects may want to use this differentiation when reporting or maintaining the information. The higher priority risks and issues are those that are mapped towards the right of the UIM. Choices as to how to prioritise risks and issues within a column will depend upon whether the assessment being undertaken is more concerned with uncertainty or known effects.

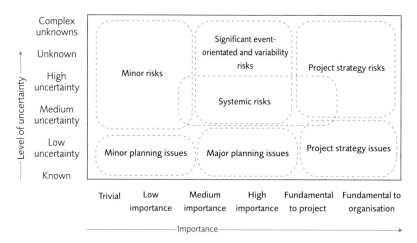

Figure 4.13 Characteristic regions in an uncertainty–importance matrix

4.2.5 High-level risk models
Purpose and applicability

Some organisations use information on generic risks to evaluate the relative risk exposure of projects as part of their strategic decision-making and portfolio management strategy. While the primary purpose of this approach may be to produce a first-pass evaluation of overall risk, a potential by-product of this approach is a project-specific prioritised listing of generic risks. As a prioritisation technique, this approach is at its most effective during the earliest phases of a project and the first pass of a risk management process.

Description

High-level risk models of this nature take on a variety of forms, but generally require the following five steps for their development.

1. Identify major sources of project risk pertinent to a project or organisation.
2. Assess the relative importance of each source and assign a weighting.
3. Define a scale against which risk levels can be assessed.
4. Assess the level of risk involved in the project in relation to each source.
5. Calculate the weighted score for each source.

Assigning weighting to risk sources and defining the scale against which risk levels are assessed are critical parts of this process. While there are a number of different methods for doing this, approaches that are not rooted in learned experience are unlikely to produce reliable results.

36

Example

Fifteen generic sources of risk are identified by an organisation as being important to its projects. Lessons learned from its previous projects are used to assign weightings. Table 4.9 shows five sources of risk, together with their weightings and an assessment of the level of risk for a particular project.

Table 4.9 Scoring of high-level generic risks

Risk sources	Weighting	Risk level	Score
1 Strategic fit (the risk of operating outside an agreed strategy)	10	0.1	1.0
2 Expertise (the risk of not having the right sort of expertise for the project)	2	1.0	2.0
3 Demands of customer (unreasonable expectations or requirements)	2	0.5	1.0
4 Planning timescale (the time pressure to make decisions and to deliver)	8	1.0	8.0
5 Maturity of project management processes (lack of proven process effectiveness and efficiency) etc.	4	0.2	0.8

In this example, Table 4.9 identifies planning timescales as being the greatest source of risk among the five shown.

Note:

1. High-level models of this nature may be developed either for a single project or for assessing all projects of a certain type owned by an organisation.
2. In the case of models constructed for single projects, the risks involved would be described in project-specific terms.
3. Some organisations use learned experience from previous projects to maintain knowledge bases that can be interrogated by high-level models of this nature.

Reference

Harris, E.P. (2007) How Managers Construe Risk in Business Acquisitions, *International Journal of Risk Assessment & Management,* Volume 7, Issue 8, pp. 1057–1073.

4.3 PRIORITISING RISKS USING QUANTITATIVE MODELS

4.3.1 Prioritisation techniques based on quantitative modelling

The risk prioritisation methods described in this section are risk and uncertainty modelling techniques that combine the implications of risks, including all relevant dependence, up to and including an analysis of total overall project risk. Typically such modelling is done with two end purposes in mind:

- gaining insights into the importance and relevance of risks with a view to better management of the project;
- obtaining unbiased forecasts of project outcomes.

The first of these purposes can be related to the prioritisation of both risks and management responses. The second may be concerned with forecasts based on either current project plans or plans changed to incorporate risk responses.

While quantitative risk modelling has become more common in project management, there remains a significant gap between common practice and best practice. A crucial factor often missing from common practice is the use of an iterative approach that commences from a high-level understanding of the effects of risk. (Figure 4.14 shows the iterative process recommended by

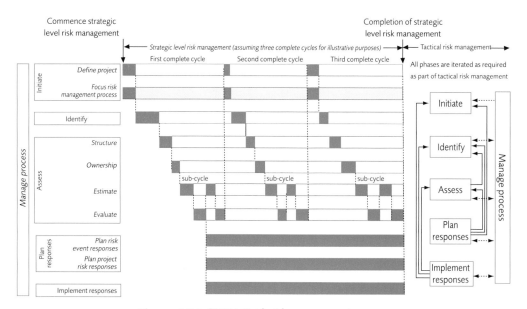

Figure 4.14 *PRAM Guide* risk management process

the *PRAM Guide*.) Instead, common practice is frequently characterised by a one-pass process based on mapping a detailed risk register onto project plans. Such approaches are liable to underestimate the effects of risk and thus undermine all the purposes of an analysis, including prioritisation.

Addressing project risk requires a holistic approach. Usually this means an integration of qualitative and quantitative analysis: some things are usefully measured in probabilistic terms, some are not. Purely qualitative holistic approaches can be relevant, addressing forms of contract, for example, or seeking understanding about interdependencies. Sometimes quantitative analysis is an end goal, but it does not have to be reached. If 'show-stopper' risks or associated feedback loops are identified, they may need resolution before any further analysis is worthwhile.

By starting from simple high-level models, a project will be able to identify key features of project risk that indicate the direction that further modelling should take and the structures that it should use. This principle lies at the heart of the iterative nature of the *PRAM Guide* process. It is also embedded in Lichtenberg's approach to risk estimation using 'the successive principle' (Lichtenberg, 2000).

A risk analyst should use 'simplicity efficiency', the simplest way of obtaining the insight which current understanding suggests ought to be the next step. Typical insights include identifying new questions and sources of bias, and understanding the interactions between risks, for example, by identifying compound effects, correlation groups and feedback loops. Other insights will include the identification of the sources of risk that matter most to project objectives. For all of these reasons, earlier passes of quantitative modelling have a third purpose to add to the two listed above:

- gaining insights into composite risks with a view to iterative management of the risk management process.

This third purpose of quantitative modelling should be understood as part of a project's processes for risk prioritisation. It should influence the identification of risks for any of the prioritisation processes described in this guide.

References

APM (2004) *Project Risk Analysis and Management Guide*, 2nd edition, APM Publishing, High Wycombe.

Lichtenberg, S. (2000) *Proactive Management of Uncertainty Using the Successive Principle*, Polyteknisk Press, Copenhagen.

4.3.2 Simple quantitative models

Purpose and applicability

Simple (or minimalist) quantitative models provide a useful first-pass approach to analysing overall project risk. They may also be useful for analysing a specific risk or response later in the project life-cycle. The aim is to provide the minimum viable level of insight with the least effort or cost. However, the insights obtained are often sufficiently important to direct the structure of more complex risk models as they are developed.

Description

1. Decompose the risk that is to be analysed into the minimum viable number of component sources of uncertainty. Usually, these will be composite risks; it is recognised that future passes of risk analysis will be based on further decomposition.
2. Use 10th and 90th percentile value estimates (P10 and P90 values) to define the spread and location of the range of possible values, while avoiding complications and bias associated with lower probability extremes.
3. Assume uniform probability density functions. The simplicity of this assumption implies that expected values are defined by the median (P50). This helps to control bias that might, for example, have been produced by anchoring estimates from a preconceived expected value.
4. Assume that there is perfect positive correlation between each of the components in the model. This is the most prudent assumption that can be made for modelling purposes and makes manual calculation easy. It implies that the extreme ends of component probability distributions can be combined to calculate the corresponding overall extreme outcome. More generally, all percentile values can be combined, useful if P10 and P90 values are added in a tabular format.
5. Portray the component composite risks using layered cumulative probability distributions whenever this is helpful, in a hierarchy which helps to clarify the structure of uncertainty components, or use a tabular equivalent.
6. Portray any associated choices using cumulative probability distributions.

Example

Figure 4.15 is based on a simplified version of a computer supplier's costing for bidding approach to systems integration projects. It portrays a cumulative probability view of the supplier's cost uncertainty using four base-level composite risk components. *A* is hardware, for which, in this example, the costs are known. *B* is software, *C* is installation, and *D* is customer staff training. In contrast to *A*, the costs for *B*, *C* and *D* are uncertain. The higher-level composite

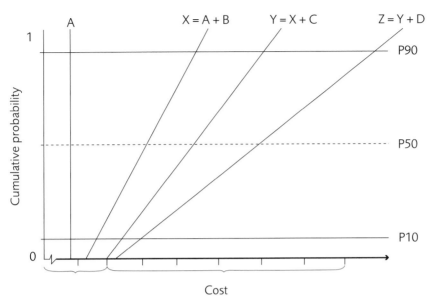

Figure 4.15 Example layered cumulative probability distribution portrayals

$X = A + B$ adds P10 and P90 values for B to the fixed value of A. In the same way the higher-level composites Y and Z continue the accumulation process by combining P10 and P90 values. The components are combined in any convenient order, starting with the fixed price component A being useful, for example. The X line shows B adds significant expected cost (by the gap from the A line on the P50) and significant variability (by the slope change/relative gaps on the P10 and P90). Expected value and variability contributions for C and D can be read from the Y and Z lines in a comparable manner.

Figure 4.16 shows the probability density function components B to D, relative to the fixed value of component A. Each probability density function has been derived from the P10 and P90 values, although for simplicity these have been shown only for component B.

Figures 4.15 and 4.16 have different advantages. Figure 4.16 may be useful to clarify how to read Figure 4.15 for those more used to probability distributions. For example, the large variability contribution of component B is illustrated by the relatively large spread between its P10 and P90 values. In contrast, component A is not subject to risk, despite having the greatest expected value.

Figure 4.15 shows the same information. Further, it shows how components accumulate to produce overall project risk. Further still, this feature can embrace the whole of project risk in a nested structure. For example, assuming Z is project risk, the components B, C and D might each have underlying

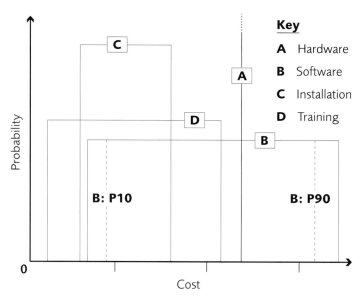

Figure 4.16 Probability density functions used in Figure 4.15

graphs comparable to Figure 4.15 showing two to six components, each of which might have further underlying graphs, and so on, with no limit to the number of risks considered in a structured integrated manner.

In addition, a variant of the format of Figure 4.15 can be helpful in supporting choices, thus providing a prioritisation focus on risk responses at any appropriate level within the nested project risk structure. For example, component *B* might be associated with choices. The *B* component of Figure 4.15 is portrayed as *B1* on Figure 4.17, shifting the probability axis to *A*'s position. *B1* to *B3* portray the cost uncertainty associated with three possible subcontractors who might be used for *B*. The *B1* choice is clearly the risk-efficient choice because its line is entirely to the left of the others. If *B1* was no longer available, the choice between *B2* and *B3* involves a trade-off between expected outcome and risk. *B3* would offer the lowest expected outcome, so would be the better choice if the marginally higher risk is acceptable from a corporate perspective. Components *A*, *C* and *D* might also involve choices, either individually or in combination, and lines comparable to Figure 4.17 might be used.

Reference

Chapman, C.B. and Ward, S.C. (2002) *Managing Project Risk and Uncertainty: A Constructively Simple Approach to Decision Making*, John Wiley, Chichester.

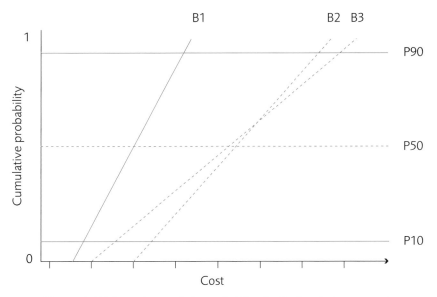

Figure 4.17 Example cumulative probability distribution choice portrayals

4.3.3 Increasing detail and complexity in quantitative risk models

Simple quantitative models such as those described in Section 4.3.2 provide a useful means of explaining some principles of risk and risk response prioritisation. However, they are often not the end point for quantitative modelling, but rather a pathway through to models with greater detail and/ or complexity. Later passes of a risk management process may develop a quantitative risk model in a number of different ways, including:

- the use of Monte Carlo simulation to consider statistical dependence levels less than 100% (coefficients of correlation less than 1), or the use of more complex dependence modelling, including conditional specifications and causal models – when simulation is introduced a number of other complexities become fairly simple;
- the use of more complex probability density functions, e.g. replacing uniform distributions with common interval rectangular histograms, or beta or triangular distributions;
- decomposing composite risks into a lower level of definition, for example into number of variability and ambiguity (threat and opportunity) risks;
- structuring models to support choices to be made between different project options;

- using probabilistic branching to simulate mutually exclusive possibilities;
- using conditional branching to simulate the effect of fallback responses;
- simulating the effects of feedback loops (e.g. modelling systemic risks with a system dynamics model);
- layering models to simulate compound risk effects where they could occur.

Choosing where to add detail and/or complexity to a risk model should be based on the priorities identified by previous passes of the risk management process. The most efficient risk management processes will focus on what aspects of risk make the most difference.

Choosing how to add detail and/or complexity is addressed by how a model is structured. A key reason for starting a quantitative risk management process with the simplest possible model is to build sound structures iteratively, thus ensuring that overall risk continues to be calculated on a rational basis. Without such an approach, detailed risk models can appear to be plausible despite being irrational and thus incorrect.

The next sections provide a range of examples that illustrate how these ideas can be applied to a number of risk modelling techniques:

- Section 4.3.4: a model of component risks within an activity/cost item;
- Section 4.3.5: a schedule risk analysis (SRA);
- Section 4.3.6: a net present value model;
- Section 4.3.7: a simple project risk re-estimating model developed from a portfolio perspective.

These examples have also been chosen to illustrate different approaches to risk and response prioritisation.

4.3.4 Component risks within an activity/cost item

Purpose and applicability

Cost risk modelling generally serves two purposes. The first is to provide an unbiased estimate of the financial contingencies required to provide an acceptable level of confidence in the overall project budget. The second is to develop a better understanding of risks in order to identify and prioritise responses that improve the project's financial outcome.

Description

It is not possible to be prescriptive about how a cost risk model should be structured. Different combinations of approaches to developing detail and structure, listed in Section 4.3.3, are appropriate in different situations. The example below is a Monte Carlo risk analysis that combines a number of features designed to add detail and complexity where it was found to be appropriate to the circumstances of the project involved. These include:

- considering the duration of the activity, defining a cost item in terms of component risks before building a cost model on top (this example concentrates on the duration aspect);
- development of rectangular histograms with 10 to 20 classes to estimate effects of each composite risk – this level of risk density function definition is responsible for the smooth appearance of the model outputs;
- use of correlation to simulate the effect of underlying interdependencies between risk outcomes;
- layering of risks in the order that makes sense from a dependency perspective – layering allows the knock-on effects of earlier risks to be simulated in later ones.

The example also includes notes of the key assumptions, an important feature of any quantitative model.

Example

Figure 4.18 shows the output of a risk model developed for a BP North Sea project. It shows incrementally the cumulative impact of six composite risks on the duration of the fabrication of the jacket (platform) for an offshore project. For example, curve 3 shows the combined effect of composite risks 1, 2 and 3. Risk 5 has the greatest impact on the project, indicated by the widest gap between the curves, and risk 2 the least. The gap associated with risk 5 portrays a significant shift in expected outcome (movement to the right) and a significant increase in variability (flattening of the curve, and lengthening of the right-hand tail). This suggests that further risk management effort should prioritise risk 5, while risk 2 should be a low priority.

In this case effort directed at risk 5 involved seeking data to test both the 'sizing' of this source of uncertainty and the presumed response – 'tight contract conditions'. The data analysis confirmed the size was about right, but it revealed the presumed response would not be effective. All observed industrial disputes occurred during the last 10% of the contract when no follow-on contracts were in place: the workforce was holding projects to ransom when it seemed there was nothing to lose. The contract terms therefore seemed irrelevant. The response to this insight was a collaborative approach by a number of oil companies to smooth their demands on yards, in part to reduce industrial disputes, in part to get better prices – a 'win–win' approach to opportunity management.

Often this approach considers a sequence of activities, modelling the accumulating impact of earlier activity delays on following activities, and 'general

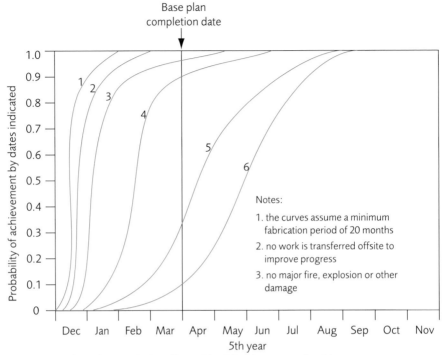

Figure 4.18 Layered risk model

responses' (not specific to individual risk events) which allow catch-up which reduces the risk of accumulated delay, but increases cost risk. The interaction between time and cost risk is part of the systemic risk structure which needs consideration, whether or not it is formally modelled.

Reference

Chapman, C.B. and Ward, S.C. (2003) *Project Risk Management: Processes, Techniques and Insights, 2nd* edition, John Wiley, Chichester, ch. 8.

4.3.5 Schedule risk analysis

Purposes and applicability

Schedule risk analysis (SRA) is a technique for analysing overall project schedule risk. It can be used to help develop project strategy by setting schedule objectives that determine realistic targets, while identifying the level of schedule contingencies needed to provide confidence that commitments will be met. Outputs from the analysis can also prioritise activities and risks in accordance with their contribution towards overall schedule risk. The approach discussed in Section 4.3.4 could be embedded in the approach of this section, which concentrates on activity relationships instead of composite risks within an activity.

Description

A network of scheduled activities and project risks is developed to form the basis of a risk model. The starting basis for this network should be a sequence of key milestones selected using a first-pass risk modelling approach analogous to the simple modelling approach described in Section 4.3.2. Typically, key milestones are selected on the basis that they represent points at which parallel work streams either are initiated or converge. They may also reflect points that lessons from previous projects suggest to be subject to risk. The network can become more detailed with successive passes of risk analysis, but should avoid the trap of breaking down activities to the point where activity dependencies become uncertain or where the quality of risk estimating is diluted by the number of estimates.

Estimates of activity duration are made using continuous probability distributions. These estimates reflect the effects of variability risk and/or composite risks. Estimates are also made for event risks to simulate their probability of occurrence and the variability of their impact, should the risk occur. Unless risks can be and have been defined in a way that makes their outcomes truly independent, correlation inputs should be used to simulate covariance in between risk outcomes. Monte Carlo simulation is used to run the SRA model to produce forecasts in a form shown by Figure 4.19.

Example

Figure 4.19 is based on the case of the final design, construction and commissioning of a naval ship. The SRA model was developed during a risk-reduction phase for the ship and commences at the main project authorisation point. The level of detail shown is equivalent to that of a second or third pass of the risk analysis process. The forecasts show that among the six key milestones, it is

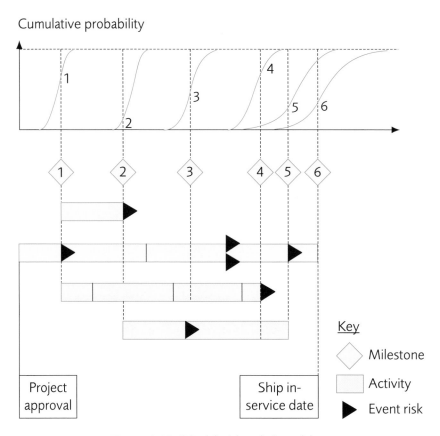

Figure 4.19 Schedule risk analysis model

milestone 2 that is most likely to be subject to delay. In this example, milestone 2 was the planned date to start cutting steel, a date dictated by resource scheduling at a particular dockyard. In effect, the analysis identified the importance of a project strategy risk caused by commercial pressure to commence manufacture without a sufficiently mature design.

Figure 4.19 also shows that schedule between milestones 4 and 5 is exposed to risk. The affected activities concerned final commissioning and inspections. Resolving the causes of risks to milestones 2 and 5 became a focus for the next pass of project planning and risk analysis.

Subsequent passes of project planning and risk analysis can also be influenced by prioritising attention on those activities and risks that statistics from the Monte Carlo analysis identify as having the greatest degree of influence over schedule variability. The properties listed in Section 4.3.9 are often used for this purpose.

4.3.6 Net present value risk model

Purpose and applicability

Net present value (NPV) risk models are appropriate to projects that involve relevant cost or benefit flows over an extended time period. Benefits can be compared with costs to determine the extent to which the business cases can be supported in terms of having a positive economic value. NPV calculations discount the value of all forecast cost and benefit values to deal with differences in the phasing of costs and benefits. NPV models may also be useful when choosing between project options (using curves for decision-making in a similar way to that shown in Figure 4.17). The models discussed in Sections 4.3.4 and 4.3.5 could be embedded in the model of this section, which concentrates on the NPV structure.

Description

As with other quantitative models, the foundation of an NPV model should be identified with a simple first-pass risk analysis. This identifies the minimum number of components required to simulate costs and benefits. In the example below, the first-pass analysis would have identified construction cost, construction duration and operating costs and revenue to be separate components. This would have prompted the identification of further key risks to be added to the model at the level of detail described (which is typical of a second-pass analysis).

The other feature of this example is the use of sensitivity analysis to prioritise risks. In contrast to the dependency layering shown in the previous examples, this process involves starting with the forecast for overall risk and then switching off one risk in turn.

Example

A project to construct a new road bridge is in the early stages of a feasibility study. The sponsor is concerned about whether or not the project can be expected to generate a positive financial return. The risk analyst responds to this question by developing an NPV risk model. This simulates the NPV for construction and revenue over a 15-year period. The model simulates the variables shown in Table 4.10.

Results from this first-pass analysis are shown in Figure 4.20. The solid curve shows the results for the combined effect of all eight sources of risk. The two dashed curves show the same data, but with the effect of one of the risks removed in each case by running the model with a fixed value instead of the input probability distribution. This shows the relative sensitivity of overall risk

Table 4.10 Inputs to a first-pass NPV model for a road bridge

Risk	Type of risk	Effect/notes
Construction cost	Composite risk	Cost of project delivery phase
Construction duration	Composite risk	Longer construction period would delay revenue; risk is correlated with construction costs
Geological conditions	Event risk	Discovery of adverse conditions could increase construction costs
Planning approval	Event risk	Planning issues arise – delay to revenue stream and/or the scope of construction.
Charge per vehicle	Variability risk	Key revenue driver
Vehicles per day	Variability risk	Key revenue driver is dependent upon utilisation; risk is inversely correlated with charge per vehicle
Operating costs	Composite risk	Costs of manning and maintenance
Interest rates	Variability risk	Value of interest rates relative to inflation influences financial return in real terms

to each of the risks in turn. On the basis of this analysis, the risk associated with the number of vehicles using the bridge per day is higher than the risk associated with operating costs.

In the above example, cruciality results from the Monte Carlo simulation could also be used to prioritise risks (see Section 4.3.9). However, for reasons explained in that section (and for risk prioritisation purposes only), it would be advisable to remove correlation from the input data.

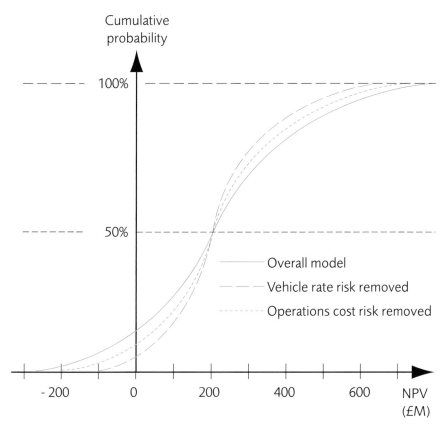

Figure 4.20 Sensitivity analysis conducted using a first-pass risk model

4.3.7 Simple project risk re-estimating model developed from a portfolio perspective

Purpose and applicability

This example illustrates how a large number of projects can be assessed rapidly within the context of a portfolio. A key feature of the analysis is that it differentiates between common sources and project-specific sources of risk. This simplifies the analysis of individual projects, thus helping achievement of a key purpose: obtaining unbiased estimates at the project level. It also helps to differentiate between responses that can be applied at an organisational level and project-specific responses. In so doing it clarifies issues of risk ownership within the organisation. Again, features associated with earlier sections, 4.3.4 to 4.3.6 in this case, could be embedded, but this example takes a simple model approach directly linked to the Section 4.3.2 approach.

Description

A simple risk model is developed using principles similar to that illustrated in Figure 4.15 but designed to estimate the effects of risk on a significant cost variable that is common to all projects.

Example

The first stage of the implementation of the 'Review of Highways Agency's Major Roads Programme' (Nichols, 2007) involved re-estimating the whole portfolio of Highways Agency (HA) projects in two months. Simplicity was critical because of the timescale, so a minimalist approach was adopted as a starting position. The key purpose of the re-estimation was to address optimism bias resulting from uncertainty excluded from previous estimates.

Sources of uncertainty having a common effect on all projects were analysed at a portfolio level. Examples included pre-construction delays for funding reasons, pre-construction inflation and anticipated changes in general design standards driven by HA policy or EU regulation. These sources of uncertainty were excluded from consideration at a project level.

A sample of projects was used to scale the whole population of projects. Each project cost within the sample was decomposed into about 10 common broad item categories, such as 'contractor's construction cost', 'traffic management' and 'land costs'.

For each project in the sample the contractor's construction cost was estimated by responsible HA staff using the process illustrated in Figure 4.21. This process was the outcome of a first-pass risk reestimation process and can be compared to Figure 4.15. In this case A was the current base estimate produced earlier by the estimators, a point value estimate; B was 'estimation uncertainty' (passing through the same P50 if appropriate provision and zero contingency for estimating error were built into the original estimate); C was 'the joint effect of all sources of uncertainty in the risk registers used previously' (with its P50 shifted to the right by an amount equal to the previous risk allowance point estimate if contingency and provision for risk register events were fully e d); and D was 'the joint effect of all other sources of uncertainty specific to this project which a minister could reasonably hold the HA accountable for' (such as the impact of reasonably foreseeable changes in EU safety rules with specific impacts not accounted for at a portfolio level).

The B to D components were estimated in cumulative form successively, not separately, and then summed. That is, HA staff located the A and B curves, then thought about the shift necessary to define the C line before finally thinking about the shift necessary to define the D curve. In this case prioritising sources of uncertainty involved estimation issues initially, ordering sources of uncertainty to clarify thinking during the estimation process. In this case the compos-

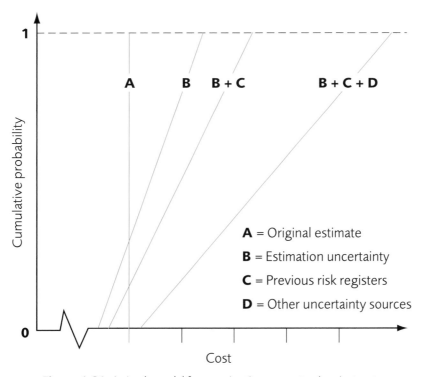

Figure 4.21 A simple model for re-estimating contractors' project costs

ite risk *C* was the total of all common practice event risks considered previously, plus the implications of dependence between them. In practice, the composite risks *B* and *D* proved to be important composite risks previously ignored, leading to persistent estimation bias.

At the next level up, the contractor's construction cost for each project was added to the other components – cost of land, cost of traffic management, and so on.

For each project within the sample, the re-estimation displayed in the form of Figure 4.21 provides a first-pass view of where the greatest sources of risk relative to current estimates lie. For example, Figure 4.21 shows that risk related to previous risk registers (component *C*) are less significant than risk related to other uncertainty sources (components *B* and *D*). Further to this, understanding the sources of uncertainty involved in each composite risk is central to prioritising. For example, a 'no design as yet' uncertainty requires different response considerations from uncertainty sources which might be reduced via immediate data acquisition or immediately developing pre-emptive management responses.

Reference

Nichols, M. (2007) *Review of Highways Agency's Major Roads Programme: Report to the Secretary of State for Transport*, Nichols Group, London.

4.3.8 Influence diagrams and system dynamics

Purpose and applicability

Influence diagrams can support the approaches to analysis discussed in the previous subsections. However, they can be used somewhat differently, leading to quite different system dynamics quantitative models.

The act of developing a cause-map of sources of uncertainty using influence diagrams rather than simply listing them in a risk register provides a number of benefits. Simply by drawing up a map and thinking about the contents, the knock-on effects of risks can be included in the considerations. Often the combination of effects can become more than the sum of their individual parts. Insights developed from this understanding are an important feature of quantitative risk modelling, particularly on complex projects. Influence diagrams are therefore a particularly useful technique for understanding the relatedness of risks.

Simple approaches to risk analysis may also result in the neglect of systemic risks. In contrast, an analysis of the effect of feedback loops enabled by the related technique of system dynamics provides a means of quantifying their effect and ranking them in terms of relative importance.

Description

This section considers a family of techniques, so space prohibits a more detailed description of each possibility. In terms of their application for risk prioritisation purposes, the most common approaches are to use quantitative models to produce sensitivity or cruciality analysis results; high values for either sensitivity or cruciality indicate the highest priority risks.

Example

Figure 4.22 illustrates a simple system dynamics model for delivering the design stage of a project. 'Stocks' are represented by square boxes and 'flows' by arrows. The circles represent the effects of risk on the design process. These can be modelled as being variability risks (such as the time or cost to complete the design) or project risks (such as the probability that a redesign will be required, and the impact that this would have). A key point is that risk effects can be modelled as being feedbacks. If there are positive feedback loops, the model may identify significant sources of system risk.

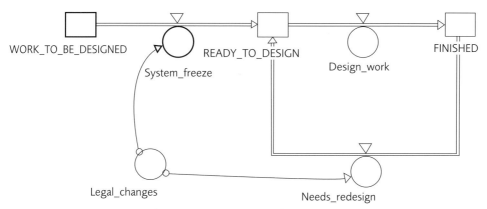

Figure 4.22 Simple system dynamics model for the design stage of a project

Reference

Williams, T. (2002) *Modelling Complex Projects*, John Wiley, Chichester.

4.3.9 Monte Carlo output statistics

Purpose and applicability

Monte Carlo simulation is the most commonly used process to operate the more complex models described in Section 4.3. In addition to its use with respect to earlier subsections, the following properties can be calculated from the Monte Carlo simulation process:

- cruciality;
- criticality (schedule risk modelling only);
- the schedule sensitivity index (schedule risk modelling only).

Risks and activities can be prioritised by listing them by a descending order of any of these three properties. Cruciality is often used as a first-choice measure for this purpose. However, realistic risk-based forecasting usually requires correlation between risks to be included as a part of the modelling process. Since the calculation of cruciality is itself based on correlation, the prioritisation of some risks by cruciality results can be misleading. Minor risks may have high cruciality values that are attributable to their association with a single major risk only, as a consequence of correlation values entered as input data. In such cases, criticality and schedule sensitivity index values may be preferred.

Description

Cruciality is the correlation between the values simulated for any element in the model and the values simulated for the model's output. The cruciality may range from 1 (perfect positive correlation) to -1 (perfect negative correlation). A cruciality of 0 indicates that the outcome of that element of the Monte Carlo model is irrelevant to the model's output.

Criticality is defined as the percentage of simulation iterations in which an activity or risk lies on the schedule critical path. The criticality of any activity in the model may range from 100% to 0. A value of 0 indicates that the outcome of the activity duration has no effect on the overall duration of the project. The criticality of a risk cannot exceed the probability of the risk's occurrence.

The schedule sensitivity index (SSI) for any activity or risk in the schedule risk model is calculated by the formula:

$$\text{SSI} = \frac{\text{Standard deviation for duration} \times \text{Criticality}}{\text{Standard deviation for the model output}}$$

It should be noted that standard deviations should be calculated from the whole of each probability distribution, including the zero duration values obtained during iterations in which a risk does not occur. The SSI formula is analogous to the simple approach of calculating the value of a risk by multiplying its probability and impact. Dividing by the standard deviation for the model's output serves the purpose of normalising the calculation.

Example

Monte Carlo prioritisation results are often presented in the form of a tornado chart. Figure 4.23 shows an example based on cruciality results produced by an intermediate level net value risk model for an offshore industry project. The highest risks are those associated with revenue : risks attributable to uncertainty in oil prices and the field's recoverable reserves. The risks associated with capital and operating costs are significant, but not as high. These insights would be of importance to the project sponsor since they could influence both the project strategy and its authorisation.

References

APM (2004) *Project Risk Analysis and Management Guide*, 2nd edition, APM Publishing, High Wycombe.

Williams, T. (2002) *Modelling Complex Projects*, John Wiley, Chichester.

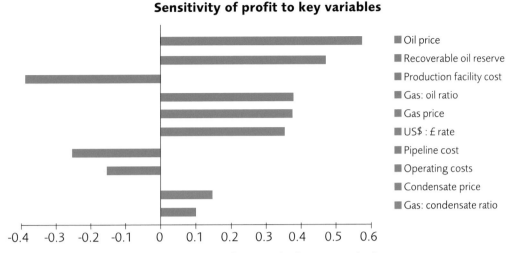

Sensitivity of profit to key variables

Figure 4.23 Illustration of prioritised risks in a tornado diagram

4.3.10 Links with other risk prioritisation techniques

A common theme of this section is that best practice requires a top-down approach to the development of quantitative risk models. In early passes of risk analysis, most modelling will be concerned with composite risks. Even when decomposition has resulted in the identification of individual event risks, variability risks, ambiguity risks and systemic risks are also likely to be important.

Some approaches to prioritising risks covered in Sections 4.1 and 4.2 are more easily aligned with best practice quantitative analysis than others. In particular, it should be noted that composite risks can involve event, variability, ambiguity and systemic risks. As a consequence, risk management approaches that use only an event-based 'threat or opportunity' approach to risk prioritisation, e.g. the probability–impact matrix, will find their risk data for the purposes of quantitative risk modelling is missing vital components, as demonstrated throughout Section 4.3.7. In contrast a technique such as the probability–impact picture is better adapted to this purpose.

5
Implications for practice

This guide shows that an understanding of the purpose of prioritisation *at the current stage in the project* is the first step to effective prioritisation, and that this purpose varies from one stage to another and from one stakeholder to another. Developing and prioritising responses may also be one of the purposes of risk prioritisation.

The second step is to understand all the elements of uncertainty and risk, not only the effects of individual risk events, but also the sources (or causes) of risk and uncertainty, and any interdependencies between them.

One or more of the techniques described in Section 4 can then be selected to prioritise as required. Some techniques may require the gathering of additional attributes or more detailed numerical information, such as three-point estimates of duration or cost. The time and cost of this additional work should be considered to ensure that it is justified and that a simpler or quicker technique will not provide the required results.

To assist in choosing a technique Table 5.1 maps the techniques in Section 4 to the seven questions described in Table 3.1.

It is tempting to believe that risk prioritisation can be achieved using the same technique in the same way in all cases. After all, risk prioritisation should enable the development of a prioritised set of risks or responses as quickly possible, so that those priorities can then be applied to the set of risk analysis and management tasks still to be done. However, if the purpose of risk prioritisation is not clear, or the definition of risk too narrow, then the result will be inappropriate priorities, lack of focus on what really matters, and the omission of potentially significant areas of risk and uncertainty. Taking a little time to clarify the purpose of prioritisation and understand risk in the wider sense of uncertainty that matters to the project will lead to an appropriate choice of tools and improved management of risk.

Table 5.1 Applicability of risk prioritisation techniques

Prioritisation techniques (see Section 4)	Prioritisation questions (see Table 3.1)						
	1 What is the current situation?	2 What needs to be done and why?	3 Do we want to do it?	4 What would we do and how (high level)?	5 What will we do and how (detail)?	6 Are we doing it right?	7 How well did we do?
4.1.1 Probability – impact picture	✓	✗	✓	✓	✓	✓	✗
4.1.2 Probability – impact matrix	✓	✗	✗	O	✓	✓	O
4.1.3 PIM extension using sliding windows	✓	✗	✗	O	✓	✓	✗
4.1.4 Expected value	✓	✗	✗	✓	✓	✓	✗
4.1.5 EV + Standard deviation (combined with E.V)	✓	✗	✓	✓	✓	✓	✗
4.2.1 Generalised (multi-attributes)	✓	✗	✗	✓	✓	✓	✗
4.2.2 Bubble chart	✓	✗	✗	O	✓	✓	✗
4.2.3 Risk prioritisation chart	✓	✗	✗	O	✓	✓	✗
4.2.4 Uncertainty– importance matrix	✓	✓	✓	O	✗	✗	O
4.2.5 High-level risk models	O	✗	✓	✓	✗	✗	✓
4.3.2 Simple quantitative models	✓	✓	✓	✓	✗	✗	✗
4.3.4–4.3.7 Intermediate/complex quantitative models	✓	✓	✓	✓	O	O	✗
4.3.8 Influence diagrams/ system dynamics	✓	✓	✓	✓	✓	✓	✓
4.3.9 Monte Carlo output statistics	✓	O	✓	✓	✓	✓	✗

Key : ✓ – common applicability; **O** – occasional applicability; **X** – weak or no applicability.